D1318603

Number Patterns at My Lemonade Stand

by Andrew Einspruch

Real World Math Books are published by Capstone Press,
151 Good Counsel Drive, P.O. Box 669, Mankato, Minnesota 56002.
www.capstonepress.com

Books published by Capstone Press are manufactured with paper
containing at least 10 percent post-consumer waste.

Library of Congress Cataloging-in-Publication Data
Einspruch, Andrew.
  Number patterns at my lemonade stand / by Andrew Einspruch. -- 1st hardcover ed.
     p. cm. -- (Real world math)
  Includes index.
  ISBN 978-1-4296-5187-5 (lib. bdg.)
  1. Lemonade--Marketing--Juvenile literature. 2. Business mathematics--Juvenile literature.
  3. Problem solving--Juvenile literature. I. Title. II. Series.

  TX911.3.M33E36 2009
  641.3'4334--dc22

2009051371

Editorial Credits
Sara Johnson, editor; Emily R. Smith, M.A.Ed., editorial director; Sharon Coan, M.S.Ed., editor-in-chief;
Lee Aucoin, creative director; Rachelle Cracchiolo, M.S.Ed., publisher

Photo Credits
The author and publisher would like to gratefully credit or acknowledge the following for permission
to reproduce copyright material: cover Pearson Education Australia/Alice McBroom Photography;
p.1 Big Stock Photo; p.4 Shutterstock; p.5 Pearson Education Australia/Alice McBroom Photography;
p.6 (top left, top right, centre and bottom right) Big Stock Photo; p.6 (bottom left) 123 Royalty Free;
p.8 (top left, middle left, and bottom) Big Stock Photo; p.8 (top right) 123 Royalty Free; p.8 (middle right)
Pearson Education Australia/Alice McBroom Photography; p.9 (top) iStock Photo; p.9 (bottom) Pearson
Education Australia/Alice McBroom Photography; p.10 iStock Photo; p.11 Pearson Education Australia/
Alice McBroom Photography; p.12 Pearson Education Australia/Alice McBroom Photography; p.14
(top) iStock Photo; p.14-15 Pearson Education Australia/Alice McBroom Photography; p.16 (top)
Photodisc; p.16 (bottom) Pearson Education Australia/Alice McBroom Photography; p.18 Pearson
Education Australia/Alice McBroom Photography; p.20 Pearson Education Australia/Alice McBroom
Photography; p.22 Pearson Education Australia/Alice McBroom Photography; p.23 iStock Photo;
p.24 Pearson Education Australia/Alice McBroom Photography; p.26 Pearson Education Australia/
Alice McBroom Photography; p.27 Big Stock Photo; p.28 Big Stock Photo; p.29 Shutterstock

While every care has been taken to trace and acknowledge copyright, the publishers tender their
apologies for any accidental infringement where copyright has proved untraceable. They would be
pleased to come to a suitable arrangement with the rightful owner in each case.

Table of Contents
Contents

How It Started

I wanted to buy a bike during summer break.
But I had no money.

Dad said he had a lemonade stand when he was a kid. It sounded like a fun idea!

Trade

If you set up a lemonade stand, then you would be known as a trader. A trader buys or sells goods.

Mom's Recipe

Mom has a great lemonade **recipe** (REH-suh-pee). It doesn't use sugar. But it uses some ginger and limes. Yum!

ginger

limes

lemons

water

honey

Mom's Lemonade Recipe

Makes about 12 pints

Ingredients:

- 4 cups honey
- about half a ginger root
- 1 gallon water
- juice of 6 lemons
- juice of 8 limes

What To Do:

1. Put the honey, ginger, and water into a big pot.
2. Ask an adult to help you bring it to a boil.
3. Ask an adult to take the pot off the stove.
   Then stir in the lemon and lime juice.
4. Let it sit and cool for half an hour.
   Then strain out the ginger.
5. Chill the drink before serving.

LET'S EXPLORE MATH

This table shows the number of lemons and limes needed to make **batches** (BAT-chez) of lemonade. Draw the table and finish the number patterns. Then answer the questions.

Number of batches	1	2	3	4	5
Lemons	6	12			
Limes	8		24	32	

a. What is the rule used to find the total number of lemons?

b. What is the rule used to find the total number of limes?

What I Will Need

Next, I have to figure out all the things I will need. I will need to buy some things.

To Buy:

- ✔ lemons
- ✔ limes
- ✔ ginger
- ✔ honey
- ✔ cups

Having Fun and Helping Others

Running a lemonade stand is fun. A lemonade stand is also a great way to raise money for your favorite **charity** (CHA-ruh-tee).

The other things I can find at home. So how much stuff should I buy? How many lemons? How many cups?

To Get from Home:
- ✔ paper and pens for signs
- ✔ table and tablecloth
- ✔ box for money
- ✔ jugs for the lemonade

How Much?

I need to figure out how many cups of lemonade I am going to sell. But who knows what that will be? I will start by working out how many batches of lemonade I will make. I think 10 batches will be enough.

If I Make 10 Batches of Lemonade:

Each batch makes 12 pints.

$$12 \text{ pints} \times 10 \text{ batches} = 120 \text{ pints of lemonade}$$

I can get cups that hold 1 pint each.

That means I will need 120 cups.

What Is a Budget?

A budget is a plan that shows how money is used over a period of time. The lemonade stand budget will show how much money is spent. It will also show how much money is made!

Now, I need to work out how much of each **ingredient** I will need to make 10 batches. Phew! That's a lot of stuff. But if I sell every cup for $1.00, I will earn $120.00. Wow!

1 Batch Needs:	10 Batches Need:
4 cups of honey	40 cups of honey
half a ginger root	5 ginger roots
1 gallon of water	10 gallons of water
6 lemons	60 lemons
8 limes	80 limes

LET'S EXPLORE MATH

Look at this table showing some of the ingredients needed to make different batches of lemonade. Draw the table and finish the number patterns.

Number of lemonade batches	2	4	6	8	10
Cups of honey		16	24		
Water (gallons)	2		6		

a. How many gallons of water do you need to make 10 batches?

b. How many cups of honey are needed to make 8 batches?

c. In the table, do the cups of honey and the water follow the same rule? Describe the rule for each pattern.

I'm in Business!

Day 1: My First Sale!

Dad helped with the shopping. He even lent me the money to pay for everything. It cost $54.00. I will pay him back when I sell some lemonade.

I made some lemonade and set up the stand. I **charged** $1.00 for a cup of lemonade.

Mr. Ling was my first customer. He liked the lemonade so much, he bought a second cup!

Day 1: Done

Today was great! I sold 70 cups and got $70.00! Dad says that is called my **income**.

LET'S EXPLORE MATH

For one batch of lemonade, you need to use 6 lemons and 8 limes. Lemons cost 10¢ each. Limes cost 15¢ each. Draw the table and finish the number patterns.

a. How much is the cost of 6 lemons?

b. How much is the cost of 8 limes?

Number of lemons and limes	1	2	3	4	5	6	7	8
Cost of lemons	10¢	20¢						
Cost of limes	15¢	30¢	45¢					

Now I need to subtract my costs. I spent $54.00 at the store. What is left over is my profit. That can go toward my bike!

Day 1: A Success!

70 cups × $1.00 per cup = $70.00 income

$70.00 income − $54.00 costs = $16.00 profit

Day 2: Ice

If I use ice, the drinks will stay cooler.
Also, it will take less lemonade to fill each cup.

I will add some ice to Mom's recipe. This means I'll get 18 cups instead of 12 per batch. So I will earn more money!

How Much Money Will I Earn if I Add Ice?

One batch of lemonade makes 12 cups.

| 12 cups | × | $1.00 per cup | = | $12.00 income |

But 1 batch + ice makes 18 cups.

| 18 cups | × | $1.00 per cup | = | $18.00 income |

LET'S EXPLORE MATH

Each cup of lemonade has 3 cubes of ice in it. Draw the table and finish the number pattern.

Number of cups	1	2	3	4	5	6
Number of ice cubes per cup		6			15	

How many ice cubes would be used in:

a. 4 cups of lemonade?

b. 6 cups of lemonade?

Day 2: Done

The ice worked. I had 50 cups of lemonade left over from yesterday. With ice, I stretched them to 75 cups. And I sold out. That is $75.00 dollars!

Dad went to the store for more cups. I had to spend money to pay for the cups. But I still made a profit.

Day 2: Lemonade + Ice = More Money!

50 cups of lemonade + ice = 75 cups of lemonade

$$75 \text{ cups} \times \$1.00 \text{ per cup} = \$75.00 \text{ income}$$

But:

$$\$75.00 \text{ income} - \$5.00 \text{ costs} = \$70.00 \text{ profit}$$

LET'S EXPLORE MATH

On Day 2, the lemonade stand made $75.00! Use this hundred chart to answer the questions.

a. Start at 7. Increase by 7 to complete the pattern all the way to the end of the chart. What numbers are in the pattern?

b. What number pattern is the blue stripe following?

1	2	3	4	5	6	7	8	9	10
11	12	13	14	15	16	17	18	19	20
21	22	23	24	25	26	27	28	29	30
31	32	33	34	35	36	37	38	39	40
41	42	43	44	45	46	47	48	49	50
51	52	53	54	55	56	57	58	59	60
61	62	63	64	65	66	67	68	69	70
71	72	73	74	75	76	77	78	79	80
81	82	83	84	85	86	87	88	89	90
91	92	93	94	95	96	97	98	99	100

Day 3: Jill Murray

I bought more stuff and made more lemonade. But now Jill Murray from school has her own lemonade stand. She will ruin my business!

I made some **flyers**. I asked Mike, my brother, to hand them out to people.

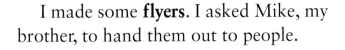

Feeling thirsty?

Come and try some ice-cold lemonade.

It's only $1 per cup!

When: today
Where: 17 Park Street

Hurry...
it's the best lemonade in town!

Day 3: Done

Jill Murray ruined my sales. I sold only 30 cups. That is less than half what I sold yesterday. But I spent more money making more lemonade! I spent $66.00 on **supplies**.

I also gave Mike $5.00 for helping with the flyers. Plus all my ice melted. I won't be able to stretch out the lemonade again. What am I going to do?

Day 3: A Bad Day

$$30 \text{ cups} \times \$1.00 \text{ per cup} = \$30.00 \text{ income}$$

But I spent $66.00 on supplies and paid Mike $5.00.

$$\$66.00 \text{ supplies} + \$5.00 \text{ to Mike} = \$71.00 \text{ costs}$$

LET'S EXPLORE MATH

It takes 12 minutes to set up my lemonade stand every day.

a. Write a number **sequence** (see-KWENZ) to show my set up time for a week.
12, 24, ___, ___, ___, ___, ___

b. Work out how many times the lemonade stand could be set up in 1 hour.

c. What rule did you follow?

Day 4: My Secret Weapon!

I had a great idea! I found a recipe on the Internet for blue lemonade. I added $5.00 worth of frozen blueberries to my **original** recipe. Result: a sell-out!

I had 120 cups left over from yesterday. The blueberries stretched that to 135 cups. But I spent $5.00 on blueberries.

Day 4

135 cups × $1.00 per cup = $135.00 income

But I spent $5.00 on blueberries.

$135.00 income − $5.00 costs = $130.00 profit

Total Income and Costs

	Income	Costs
Day 1:	$70.00	$54.00
Day 2:	$75.00	$5.00
Day 3:	$30.00	$71.00
Day 4:	$135.00	$5.00
Total:	$310.00	$135.00

$310.00 − $135.00 = $175.00 total profit!

The Best Summer Ever!

I kept my stand going all summer break. The blue lemonade was a big hit!

My stand was open 60 days in all. I sold 3,600 cups of lemonade. That's $3,600.00. After I subtracted my costs, I had $1,980.00 left over. I bought a great bike. Then I put the rest in the bank.

I am glad I set up my lemonade stand. It was great to earn money. I also learned about budgets while having fun. It was the best summer ever!

LET'S EXPLORE MATH

Draw a table to show the number pattern you would use to solve this problem. If you made 5 batches of lemonade a day, what would be the total number of batches made in:

a. 2 days?   **b.** 6 days?   **c.** 12 days?

Cars and Dolls

Dadov toy makers ship their toys around the world. Their most famous toys are trucks and dolls.

The doll makers make 5 dolls in the first hour. As they get better at making dolls, they can make 1 more doll each hour than in the previous hour.

The truck makers make 9 trucks in the first hour. Each hour, they gain 1 more worker. So, they can make 3 more trucks each hour than in the previous hour.

Solve It!

a. How many hours did the doll makers have to work to create 81 dolls?

b. How many hours did the truck makers have to work to create 75 trucks?

c. How many dolls and trucks are made after 10 hours?

Use the steps below to help you solve the problem.

Step 1: Create the chart below. Use a number pattern to work out the number of toys made every hour.

Hour	1	2	3	4	5	6	7	8	9	10
Dolls made	5	6	7							
Trucks made	9	12	15							

Step 2: Create the chart below to work out the total number of toys that the workers have at the end of each hour.

Hour	1	2	3	4	5	6	7	8	9	10
Total dolls made	5	11	18							
Total trucks made	9	21	36							

Glossary

batches—the amount of something made at one time

charged—asked as payment

charity—an organization that gives help to others

costs—amounts of money spent on a project

flyers—advertising materials, such as posters

income—an amount of money earned

ingredient—something that goes into a recipe

original—being the first of something from which other things are made

profit—the money remaining after all costs have been paid for

recipe—a list of ingredients and instructions for making a type of food or drink

sequence—a pattern following a rule; a number pattern follows a rule

supplies—goods needed

Index

Internet Sites

FactHound offers a safe, fun way to find Internet sites related to this book. All of the sites on FactHound have been researched by our staff.

Here's all you do:

Visit *www.facthound.com*

FactHound will fetch the best sites for you!

Let's Explore Math

Page 7:
a. Add 6 **b.** Add 8

Page 11:

Number of lemonade batches	2	4	6	8	10
Cups of honey	8	16	24	32	40
Water (gallons)	2	4	6	8	10

a. 10 gallons
b. 32 cups
c. No. Honey = Add 8; Water = Add 2

Page 14:

Number of lemons and limes	1	2	3	4	5	6	7	8
Cost of lemons	10¢	20¢	30¢	40¢	50¢	60¢	70¢	80¢
Cost of limes	15¢	30¢	45¢	60¢	75¢	90¢	$1.05	$1.20

a. 6 lemons cost 60¢
b. 8 limes cost $1.20

Page 17:

Number of cups	1	2	3	4	5	6
Number of ice cubes per cup	3	6	9	12	15	18

a. 36 ice cubes are used in 12 cups of lemonade.
b. 54 ice cubes are used in 18 cups of lemonade.

Page 19
a.

1	2	3	4	5	6	7	8	9	10
11	12	13	14	15	16	17	18	19	20
21	22	23	24	25	26	27	28	29	30
31	32	33	34	35	36	37	38	39	40
41	42	43	44	45	46	47	48	49	50
51	52	53	54	55	56	57	58	59	60
61	62	63	64	65	66	67	68	69	70
71	72	73	74	75	76	77	78	79	80
81	82	83	84	85	86	87	88	89	90
91	92	93	94	95	96	97	98	99	100

7, 14, 21, 28, 35, 42, 49, 56, 63, 70, 77, 84, 91, 98
b. Add 10

Page 23:
a. 12, 24, 36, 48, 60, 72, 84
There are 84 minutes of set up time each week.
b. Five lemonade stands can be set up in 1 hour.
c. Add 12

Page 27:
5 batches per day

Number of days	2	6	12
Number of batches	10	30	60

a. 10 batches **b.** 30 batches **c.** 60 batches

Page 28:

Problem-Solving Activity

Hour	1	2	3	4	5	6	7	8	9	10
Dolls made	5	6	7	8	9	10	11	12	13	14
Trucks made	9	12	15	18	21	24	27	30	33	36

Hour	1	2	3	4	5	6	7	8	9	10
Total dolls made	5	11	18	26	35	45	56	68	81	95
Total trucks made	9	21	36	54	75	99	126	156	189	225

a. The doll makers worked 9 hours to make 81 dolls.
b. The truck makers worked 5 hours to make 75 trucks.
c. After 10 hours there were 95 dolls and 225 trucks.